365 BADASS BLACK MOM AFFIRMATIONS

POSITIVE THOUGHTS TO CREATE HAPPINESS, BUILD CONFIDENCE, ENCOURAGE BONDING, AND ELIMINATE STRESS AND ANXIETY FOR PARENTS AND SINGLE MOMS

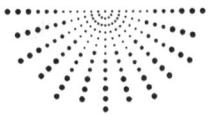

JASMINE GREENE

CONTENTS

INTRODUCTION

Hello. My name is Jasmine, and I know too well how rewarding, stressful, and overwhelming being a mom can be. It's one of those rare adventures in life that is truly magical and challenging all at once. Your complete routine, lifestyle, and identity gets flipped upside down when you have children, and unfortunately, negative emotion and thoughts can creep into your life. This happens to us all, and if we don't redirect our minds, a little hiccup can quickly turn into lasting stress and anxiety.

Over the next few chapters, we will feed your mind with powerful, positive thoughts so you can embrace the amazing mom you truly are. The more time you commit to reading and redirecting your thoughts, the quicker you will feel in control and valued as a mom.

There is no right or wrong way to use these affirmations. You can go through chronologically or jump ahead to a chapter that covers the things you are struggling with. Each one is designed to support you in a specific area of "mom life."

You are welcome to read the affirmations out loud or in your head. Depending on what life has thrown at me for a particular day, you will find me repeating affirmations to myself as I run around town doing errands, take a shower, or lie in bed. I like to pick one affirmation before I go to bed and carry it with me throughout the next day as my mantra. This reminds me that I deserve to feel valued, in control, confident, and happy as a mom no matter what happens. Make a small commitment to yourself right now to read at least one affirmation every day.

Congratulations on putting yourself first. You are now on your way to becoming a Badass Black Mom.

1
RELEASE TOXIC GUILT

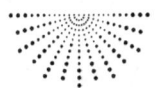

1. I show my family how much I love them by loving myself.

2. I forgive myself for being an imperfect parent.

3. I am tuned into my needs and prioritize self-care.

4. I am the best mother for my children; I was born to be their mother.

5. I make time for the things I enjoy.

6. Just as the needs of my children matter, so do my own.

7. Today I allow time for self-care and rejuvenation.

8. I deserve to put my feet up and relax.

9. I am worthy of love and admiration.

10. I take exquisite care of myself.

11. I am a brilliant, beautiful black woman.

12. I choose to take care of myself.

13. I will be kind to myself.

14. I always remember to fill my cup.

15. My goals are still important.

16. I take care of my black body, mind, and soul.

17. I love and accept myself exactly as I am.

18. I deserve time to myself.

19. I am a loving mother to my children.

20. I will take care of myself in order to be a good mother.

21. I am enough.

22. It is imperative that I take care of myself. Self care is not selfish.

23. I am more than a mother.

24. I am still capable of achieving my hopes and dreams.

25. I do not need permission to feel glorious.

26. I am doing my best as a mom and that is enough.

27. By allowing myself to be happy, I inspire my family to be happy as well.

28. I take care of myself.

29. I accept myself for who I am and am confident in my abilities.

30. My own needs are important!

31. I'm doing an amazing job!

32. I am everything my child needs.

33. I am a fantastic role model for my children.

34. I give myself permission to do something to nurture me.

35. A successful relationship with my child is not defined by what we have but by the time we spent together.

36. Taking care of myself is a responsibility I will model to my children without guilt.

37. Establishing personal boundaries and sticking to them helps me remember that I am important too.

38. I do not need to compare myself to other moms.

39. I choose to care for myself.

40. Every day I know that I am doing the best that I can.

41. I'm a good mom because I love my children.

42. I'm a great mother already, even as I work tirelessly to be a better one.

43. My dreams and desires matter and I am capable of doing amazing things.

44. I am aware that I cannot do it all and it is okay to ask for help.

45. Everything I am looking for I can find within myself.

46. I am more than just a mother.

47. It's okay to take care of myself and my needs too.

48. It is okay to say "no" to things when I am overwhelmed.

49. I forgive myself for my failures and understand I am not perfect.

50. I deserve to care for myself too.

51. I am learning to be a better mother with each new day.

52. I always give myself what I need.

53. Taking care of myself makes me a better mom.

54. I give myself permission to do something to nurture ME.

55. In the eyes, mind and heart of my child, I am a good mom.

56. Taking care of myself makes me a better mom because I parent from abundance, not from lack thereof.

57. I am a good mom, even as I work to become a better one.

58. I am the exact parent my child needs to blossom so I don't need to compare myself to others.

59. Not loving every moment of motherhood doesn't mean I don't love being a mom.

60. I get the rest I need.

61. I take the time I need to care for my own needs—doing this supports me in being a better parent.

62. I will build into myself so that I can parent from a place of rest and happiness rather than exhaustion and bitterness.

63. I have feelings that deserve to be recognized.

2
BOND YOUR FAMILY

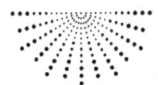

1. I act in a way that shows respect for my children.

2. My children will feel accepted and loved unconditionally by me.

3. The more I release, the more I love.

4. We stay fit and love to exercise.

5. When something is out of balance, I seek answers and am led to solutions that make a difference.

6. I do what it takes to give the best to my family.

7. Life is good in my family.

8. We have a great time together.

9. I listen to understand.

10. I am my children's rock.

11. I respect my children; I respect myself.

12. Everyone is willing to contribute to maintaining the order and function of our home.

13. I approach all disciplinary functions with a peaceful honoring tone of voice and behavior that is respectful of my child.

14. The more I love, the more I am loved.

15. Dinner is an enjoyable experience we all look forward to.

16. I see the joy in spending my day teaching and loving my children.

17. I validate my child's feelings.

18. I am learning a lot from my children.

19. All of my children feel safe and honored by me.

20. I am a good listener.

21. I find answers when something is out of balance.

22. I am unwavering in my love for my children.

23. I am my children's safe space.

24. Our family makes an extra effort to get along and be each other's good friends.

25. Though these times are difficult, they are only a short phase of life. This too shall pass.

26. My love for my children is unconditional.

27. My children come to me to share what they need support with.

28. I am using discipline appropriately in a way that helps my children correct their behavior to learn new ways of approaching things.

29. I say "tell me more" frequently.

30. My relationship with my family is becoming stronger, deeper, and more stable each day.

31. My children look up to me and recognize my worth.

32. My family's best interest is my first priority and I make my decisions with them in mind.

33. There is tremendous harmony in our family.

34. I understand that discipline is a tool to help change behavior when the behavior is not congruent with what is best.

35. I have patience.

36. My love and connection helps my child above all else.

37. I have good communication skills.

38. I help them learn through correct discipline how to optimize their true self.

39. I accept and appreciate the connection to my children

40. I love the traditions we have that support our day-to-day and holiday experiences.

3
PRIORITIZE GRATITUDE

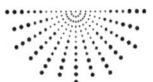

1. I love being a mom

2. I am thankful for my wonderful children.

3. Love and blessings are chasing my family down.

4. My children are healthy, creative, and loving, and I am thankful!

5. I am blessed with an incredible family and wonderful friends.

6. I am blessed with added patience when I am losing control.

7. I am grateful for the time I have with my kids today.

8. My children are blessed to have me as their mother.

9. I am grateful for the good food that my children love to eat.

10. I am thankful we stay healthy all year round.

11. I radiate beauty, charm, and grace.

12. I am blessed to be their mother.

13. My continuous hard work in motherhood is worship to the Lord.

14. I am grateful for the resources that continue to show up to help me be a great parent.

15. I am grateful for my ability to create life.

16. My home is full of love and joy.

17. My life is beautiful.

18. I appreciate my children and everything that makes them unique.

19. I am grateful for how much cooperation we experience as a family.

20. I admire my body for creating a new life.

21. It is wonderful we are all free of illness and disease.

22. It's amazing how successful our family is.

23. My children will rise up and call me blessed.

24. My thoughts are filled with positivity and my life is plentiful with prosperity.

25. My children are grateful for me.

26. Our home is a safe and peaceful haven.

27. Being a mom is a blessing.

28. I am perfectly healthy in body, mind, and spirit.

29. I am grateful for the abundance in my life.

30. God's hand is on my children's lives.

31. I am blessed with patience and understanding before I lose control.

32. I am a blessing to my family.

33. I'm grateful to spend time with my children every day.

34. My children love me and are thankful for me, even when they don't say it.

35. I am grateful for the family I have.

36. Today and every day I am enough.

37. My family appreciates and loves me, even when they forget to tell me so.

38. I am a blessing to my children.

4
TRUST YOUR INTUITION

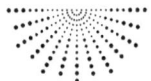

1. I trust my maternal intuition.

2. I trust the magic of divine timing.

3. Life is conspiring in my favor.

4. I am attracting the perfect situations into my life.

5. All is well. They are well and I am well.

6. Everything is exactly the way it needs to be in order to learn the lessons I need the most.

7. Everything I need comes to me at the right time.

8. Worrying about what others think only distracts me from being the parent I need to be.

9. I am in the flow of life.

10. Creative energy surges through me and leads me to new and brilliant ideas.

11. No matter what, everything is happening perfectly in my life.

12. I am a powerhouse; I am indestructible.

13. Everything that is happening now is happening for my ultimate good.

14. I trust my mother's intuition and let it guide me.

15. I let go of all self doubts and begin to trust my inner self.

16. Through God I can do all things. He has called me to motherhood.

17. Whenever I am in a doubt, I always listen to my intuition.

18. I believe in abundance.

19. My children trust me beyond measure.

20. I always know what is best for my children

21. I am raising bold, beautiful, black children.

22. I let my children be who they are.

23. I trust my intuition to guide me in the right direction at all times.

24. I am making the best decisions I can for my family.

25. I trust my parenting instincts.

26. I do not need to control my children, only gently and lovingly guide them.

27. I trust my intuition to make intentional parenting choices and decisions.

28. Everything is happening for me.

BECOME A CONFIDENT PARENT

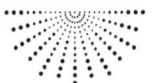

1. I draw on the support that surrounds me, in whatever form.

2. I am valuable to my family.

3. I always give my family what they need.

4. I am a badass black mom!

5. Motherhood reveals my strengths to me.

6. I am powerful and strong.

7. I am preparing my children for the world as best as I know how.

8. Being a mother has shown me how strong I am.

9. Comparisons do not serve me

10. When I compare myself to other parents, I quickly let those thoughts go.

11. My children are lucky to have such a caring, devoted mother.

12. I radiate grace, confidence, and care.

13. Today I am strong and healthy.

14. I am brave and courageous.

15. I am raising world changers.

16. I am what my child needs. Worrying about what others think only distracts me from being the parent I need to be.

17. Everything I do serves a purpose for my family.

18. My children will have the same opportunities as other children.

19. I will make the most of today.

20. Every challenge I face makes me stronger as a black mother.

21. Other mothers look up to me for advice and inspiration.

22. I am powerful beyond measure.

23. I am courageous to show my children vulnerability.

24. The best moms are the ones who struggle the most. It means they care enough to do better.

25. In the eyes, mind, and heart of my child, I am a good mom.

26. I am a loving woman who sets an amazing example for her children.

27. My children need me in their life.

28. I am confident and growing in my parenting role.

29. I am capable of amazing things if I believe it to be true and act on those feelings.

30. My spouse and I agree on healthy parenting approaches.

31. Only good lies before me.

32. I am a great mother.

33. I become a more confident mother with each new day.

34. I am brave and courageous for trying even when I think I can't do it.

35. I acknowledge my own self-worth; my confidence is soaring.

36. I am the perfect mother for my children.

37. I am capable of raising my kids.

38. I make good decisions for my children.

39. I am courageous and I stand up for myself.

40. I exude strength, grace, and flexibility.

41. I am the architect of my life; I build its foundation and choose its contents.

42. I am always doing my best as a mother.

43. Being a good mom takes courage, and today I'm feeling brave.

44. I am doing a good job.

45. My obstacles are moving out of my way; my path is carved towards greatness.

46. I am brave.

47. I will be the type of person I would like my children to become.

48. I am admired.

6
REALIZE YOUR TRUE VALUE

1. I possess the qualities needed to be fully happy.

2. I am important in the lives of my children.

3. I listen to the spirit and I am guided.

4. I am more than enough.

5. I am becoming the best version of myself.

6. I always remember to demonstrate what I expect from my children.

7. I do what is correct for me and my children.I support others in choosing the same.

8. I am raising adults who will contribute to the good of society.

9. Being a mother makes me feel beautiful.

10. Loving my children is more important than loving every moment of motherhood.

11. There is no such thing as "just a mom".

12. I am a good role model to my children on how to take care of my body.

13. My children are raised to be proud of their hair, skin tone, and body features.

14. I will show my children the world.

15. I am the exact parent my child needs to blossom.

16. Being a black mom is my super power.

17. I am raising black professionals, politicians, and leaders.

18. I enjoy food preparation and can even find resources to support me when I need a break.

19. My life is just beginning.

20. I am doing an amazing job.

21. I love being a parent.

22. The time I am investing in my children matters.

23. I show my children how to be kind, gracious, and loving.

24. I am aware of my child's nature and supportive of them living their truth.

25. I will show my children what it means to take care of yourself.

26. I teach my kids to be authentic.

27. I am willing to learn and grow.

28. I stand up for my children.

29. I create a safe environment for my children – physically, emotionally, mentally, and spiritually.

30. I am a leader to my children.

31. There's value in showing my kids my vulnerability.

32. I am black girl magic.

33. Giving my child time and attention is more important than giving them material things.

34. As I teach my kids today, I will also be open to the lessons they can teach me.

35. I release expectations and allow my children and family to be who we are.

36. I teach my black children how to be fierce and bold.

37. I am the exact mother my children need to blossom, so I do not need to compare myself to other mothers.

38. I am my child's lifelong teacher.

39. I take the necessary steps to ensure I am supporting their health and wellness.

40. I teach my children to love and respect their bodies.

41. I am everything to my children.

42. I am healthy and vibrant.

43. My children matter.

44. I teach my kids by example every day.

45. I am building wealth to leave my children an inheritance.

46. I teach my children that anything is possible for them by setting ambitious goals of my own.

47. I love how much joy this role gives me.

48. My decisions benefit my children.

49. I have been called to motherhood—the most powerful calling in the world.

50. I am raising God-fearing children who will change the world.

51. I show my children how to achieve their goals by achieving my own goals.

52. Motherhood has revealed my strengths and I am becoming a better version of myself.

53. I will show my children how to advocate for kindness and justice.

54. I am a great parent.

55. I easily make changes when change is the best option.

56. Only I can give my children a happy mother.

57. I am a role model, guide and friend to my child as their parent.

58. Motherhood is not made up of one success or failure, but rather by the sum of my parenting choices.

7

TACKLE THE DAY TO DAY

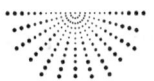

1. My children do their chores willingly.

2. I will talk about myself the way I would my best friend.

3. Peace and joy are filling my life.

4. My mothering body is beautiful

5. I know how to support there true natures by giving them jobs they can accomplish easily.

6. I will have fun doing the mundane tasks today.

7. Asking for help does not mean I'm a failure.

8. Sometimes the house will not be clean, but it is okay because I am a mother first.

9. My children's health is a priority to me and I feed my children healthy food options.

10. I am loved.

11. Happiness is a choice.

12. I forgive my children's flaws.

13. Today I am enthusiastic and full of energy

14. I have boundless energy!

15. I release judgment and embrace the present moment.

16. My children do not need me to be perfect; they just need me.

17. I am the calm in the chaos.

18. We are making fond memories with the activities we enjoy in our home.

19. We have a lot of fun in our home.

20. I'm doing a stunning job!

21. I wake up today with strength in my heart and clarity in my mind.

22. My family sees the best in me.

23. I forgive those who have harmed me in my past and peacefully detach from them.

24. I exude patience and grace throughout my day.

25. Our home is a place of peace.

26. I accomplish everything I need to to care for my children.

27. I will play with my children today.

28. My children do not care about my flaws.

29. My ability to conquer my challenges is limitless; my potential to succeed is infinite.

30. Our home is orderly and organized.

31. I will treasure my children as the unique individuals they are.

32. I will let go of how I think today is supposed to go and accept it as it comes.

33. I am lovable and deeply loved.

34. I always speak to my child in a loving, kind tone of voice.

35. A river of compassion washes away my anger and replaces it with love

36. I am powerful.

37. I smile on my flaws today.

38. Happiness is my choice.

39. I am capable of amazing things if I believe it to be true and act.

40. Today is just one day.

41. I love my children even on the days I don't particularly like them.

42. Today, I abandon my old habits and take up new, more positive ones.

43. We enjoy each other's company and know when to give each other privacy.

44. I will do my best as a mom, and that will always be enough.

45. My imperfections today are not important.

46. I will make memories with my children and ignore the dirty dishes.

47. I can communicate my needs and feelings.

48. My children will remember the time we spend together, not what they were given.

49. I do not expect to be a perfect mother.

50. Being a mom causes me joy and happiness.

51. I accept where I am in life and will make the most of today.

8

FEEL RELAXED AND IN CONTROL

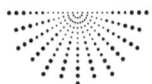

1. I have everything I need for a happy life.

2. I feel calm in the midst of chaos.

3. Today, I choose joy!

4. I will turn away from judgement today.

5. I am free of anxiety and am living a calm life.

6. One task at a time is enough.

7. I have the ability to overcome anxiety.

8. Today I will find peace in being good enough because perfection is impossible.

9. Anxiety might make me feel uncomfortable but I am in charge of my mind and body.

10. I am relaxing each part of my body.

11. Today I will let go of any guilt weighing on my shoulders.

12. I am calm and peaceful under pressure.

13. The feelings of panic are leaving my body.

14. Mistakes and setbacks are stepping stones in my motherhood journey because I learn from them.

15. My black body is calm.

16. I am ridding my mind of negative thoughts and filling it with positive ones.

17. I am in charge of how I feel today. I am choosing happiness.

18. I am doing the best I can.

19. I will accomplish everything on my list today!

20. The right decisions are coming to me easily now.

21. I can and do choose peace.

22. I will do what I can and nobody expects me to do it all.

23. I release the need for perfection.

24. I am now in control.

25. I am freeing myself from stress.

26. I will leave my expectations for today and what it should look like at the door.

27. I choose carefully what goes onto my calendar.

28. I choose to be calm and centered, regardless of the situation.

29. I am capable of solving any problems that face me.

30. I release the need to dwell on bad feelings.

31. I will let go of how I think today is supposed to go and accept how it imperfectly happens.

32. I breathe in relaxation, I breathe out tension.

33. It's going to be okay.

34. I can handle life's challenges.

35. Everything is working out for my highest good.

36. I will push through challenges so that my struggles today will become my strengths tomorrow.

37. I handle stress effortlessly!

38. My mind is clearing and I am in control.

39. All is well in my world.

40. I am never in a rush; my timing is perfect.

41. I am calmer and calmer with each deep breath I take.

42. There is peace and love in my home, even in the midst of chaos.

43. All my needs are met with ease.

44. One bad day does not make me a bad mom, only human.

45. I am safe and in control.

46. I am happy.

47. I will embrace the here and now.

48. Today I will notice the positive aspects of motherhood.

49. I am free of anything that weighs me down.

50. I handle it all with confidence and grace.

51. I am attracting positive energy into my body.

52. I breathe and relax knowing the universe supports me.

53. This too shall pass.

54. I will not worry about small details today.

55. Today I will love fiercely, laugh freely and live courageously.

56. I am at peace with all that has happened, is happening, and will happen

57. My fears of tomorrow are simply melting away.

CONCLUSION

Congratulations! You are now on your way to becoming the best mom that you can be. If you feel like this book helped you, it would be fantastic if you could leave a review on Amazon. Reviews will help this book reach other moms that need to be told they are amazing and powerful even when everything is hitting the fan. Let's get this book out there to as many moms as we can and make this world full of powerful parents. Just imagine if all black moms knew their true worth! Ah, what a pretty picture!

BONUS #1: AFFIRMATIONS FOR NEW MOMS

1. I am learning to be a better mother every day.

2. I give myself credit for all I have learned as a mom.

3. I have unlimited patience.

4. I allow others to help me with tasks.

5. I release my hesitation and make room for triumph.

6. I am focused on making my baby happy.

7. I have excellent mothering skills.

8. I'm proud of all I have accomplished.

9. I am not alone.

10. I am a strong and loving mother.

11. Being a good mom means I nurture myself and take care of my needs also.

12. I have a balanced mind, body and spirit.

13. I trust my maternal instincts.

14. Today I release expectations of perfection.

15. I am going to be a great mom.

16. I am doing a great job as a parent.

17. I love taking good care of myself for my baby and me.

18. I value my unique skills and talents.

19. I feel positive in new situations.

20. Peace comes when I let go of trying to control every tiny detail.

21. I believe in myself as a capable and wonderful mother.

22. I know that I can master anything if I do it enough times.

23. I wake up loving my life.

24. I am successful in taking care of my baby.

25. I am learning to understand my child's needs.

26. I easily adapt to the changes that new motherhood brings.

27. My inner voice guides me in every moment.

28. I exude confidence as a mother.

29. My mother's intuition leads me to the right choices.

30. Needing a break doesn't make me a bad mom.

31. I am the perfect mother for my baby.

32. I fulfill my purpose as a mother by starting here, right now.

33. I face difficult situations with courage and conviction.

34. My internal dialogue is loving, forgiving and kind.

35. I love and accept all of my thoughts and feelings.

36. I can do this.

37. I am grateful for the miracle of my body.

38. I speak kindly to myself.

39. I have the strength to take care of all of my baby's needs.

40. I know that I am the best mother I can be.

41. I choose to see the divine perfection in every part of myself.

42. My day is filled with a limitless potential of joy, happiness and love.

43. I love myself no matter what.

44. I like how I mother my baby more each day.

45. I sleep deeply and restfully every night.

46. Today I see each moment as a new opportunity to express my greatness as a mom.

47. Today I am willing to accept my imperfections.

48. I am becoming a better mother every day.

49. I cherish this time.

50. I always see the positive aspects of motherhood.

51. I am grateful for the baby in my life.

52. I love the unique mom that I am becoming.

53. I am able to easily handle any problem I face.

54. I appreciate my wonderful life more each day.

55. I grow in strength with every forward step I take into motherhood.

56. I'm proud of myself for attempting new things.

57. Today I give myself permission to be greater than my fears.

58. I am meant to be a great mother.

59. I am limited only by my vision of what is possible.

60. Today I present my love, passion, and joy to motherhood.

61. Today I put my full trust in my inner guidance.

62. My flaws are transformed by love and acceptance.

63. I trust my feelings and insights as a mother.

64. Fear is only a feeling; it cannot hold me back.

65. Today I choose to honor my strengths as a mom.

66. My baby's cries sound like music to me.

67. I am full of energy.

BONUS #2: AFFIRMATIONS FOR DIVORCED & SINGLE MOMS

1. All that I need is within me.

2. I am stronger than I was yesterday.

3. I am grateful that I have my children.

4. I have a great life regardless of my situation.

5. I am learning to laugh more.

6. God gives strength to single parents.

7. Single parents are brave.

8. I am learning to be less of a perfectionist with myself and others.

9. I find time to connect with other single moms

10. I have kind caring affordable sitters whenever I choose.

11. Being a single parent is part of what makes me unique.

12. My children and I form a strong bond.

13. I am learning to forgive my own shortcomings.

14. Everything is happening as it should be.

15. I'm brave and courageous today.

16. I am learning to be more forgiving of imperfections in others.

17. I am a beautiful person. Inside and out.

18. I am grateful for the relationship I had with my former partner.

19. I choose to be happy and hopeful even though it may seem too difficult.

20. It's okay to feel lost at times, this is only a temporary situation.

21. I am working hard to better myself physically, emotionally, and financially.

22. I have those who are willing to help when necessary.

23. I am learning to trust again, by first trusting myself.

24. If I do nothing today besides hug my kids, then I've done enough.

25. My heart is healing.

26. I am learning to be more tolerant of other opinions.

27. I am stronger than I seem. I am braver than I think.

28. I am a good person with a lot to offer.

29. I am fully capable of being alone right now and I'm okay with it.

30. Divorce is not the end of the road, it's only the beginning.

31. Change is the only constant and I will move through this with grace and ease.

32. I have an opportunity now to create the life I want.

33. I can navigate a life with my ex, we can function as partners.

34. I choose to put my children first and help them to have a stable home life.

BONUS #3: AFFIRMATIONS FOR WORKING MOMS

1. I love my children just as much as I would if I were staying at home.

2. I will be an intentional parent.

3. I am grateful to be a provider for my kids.

4. I am the best mom for my kids.

5. Today I will let go of the guilt weighing on my shoulders.

6. I will laugh and play with my children when we are together.

7. I love my children, my family and myself.

8. There is peace and love in our home.

9. It's okay to ask for help.

10. The work I do is meaningful and beneficial to others.

11. In the eyes, mind and heart of my child, I am a good mom.

12. I take excellent care of my kids.

13. I am not perfect but I am what my child needs.

14. I am more than just a mom.

15. I am strong powerful and unstoppable

16. I am a positive role model for my children

17. I am in control of my feelings.

18. I am a strong woman setting a great example for my kids.

19. Everything I do serves a purpose for my family.

20. I show up even on the bad days, because I am resilient.

21. I know my children and how to make them smile.

22. I find joy in the little everyday moments.

23. I am a great role model for my kids.

24. My love and connection helps my child above all else.

25. I will trust my intuition to guide me in the right direction at all times.

26. I practice self-care so that I'm a happier, healthier mom for my kids.

27. My days are filled with purpose and passion.

28. My children are smart, strong and caring because of my example.

29. I am doing the best I can, and that is enough.

30. I am working hard to support my family.

31. I got this!

32. Quality family time outweighs quantity.

33. I believe in myself and my motherly instincts.

34. I am calm through the chaos.

35. It's okay to not feel strong and in control at every moment.

36. I am present with my children when I'm at home.

37. I am the best mom for my children.

38. These are the best days of my life.

39. The decisions I make are in the best interest of my family.

40. I am not comparing myself to the mothers around me; I am the perfect mother for my child.

41. My work gives me skills to teach my kids.

42. I embrace imperfection.

43. Motherhood makes me more caring, compassionate and courageous.

44. I am thankful for family time at home.

45. I am doing the best I can at all times.

46. My positive thoughts and actions create positive feelings in my kids.

BONUS #4: AFFIRMATIONS FOR STAY AT HOME MOMS

1. My home is a safe place.

2. My job at home is worth millions.

3. I will take care of myself.

4. When there is chaos around me, I am the calm.

5. I will not compare my children to other children.

6. It's okay to ask for help.

7. I might not see it now but the time I'm investing in my kids does matter.

8. When they are grown, I won't remember one terrible day.

9. I am more than just a mom.

10. I will feel good about what I did accomplish today.

11. I love watching my child grow.

12. If I do nothing today besides hug my kids then I have done enough.

13. I will laugh with my children today.

14. I will do what I can; no one expects perfection.

15. This too will pass.

16. I am leaving a legacy of love.

17. I fully embrace today.

18. I try to meet every need my child has.

19. If I do happen to lose my patience, that doesn't make me a bad mom, it makes me a human being, and these things happen.

20. The decisions made by other moms do not need to dictate mine or how I feel about myself as a mother.

21. I will only let social media be an inspiration, not a reason to stress out about my lack.

22. I am a good mom.

23. My children will not remember a pristine house, they will remember the time I spent with them.

24. Being a stay at home mom is fulfilling.

25. I will never compare myself to other moms.

26. I am blessed to be me.

27. The world will not stop turning if I don't get to that mess today.

28. I enjoy being there for my children.

29. I won't beat myself up.

30. I love spending time with my children.

31. If my husband asks me what I did today I will not cry, scream or complain.

32. I have patience and understanding for my child.

33. I am a patient mom.

34. I will not allow myself to feel guilty about any decision that I make in the best interest of my child.

REFERENCES

A., B. (2021, February 3). *100 Positive Affirmations for Every Mom*. Bert Anderson · Me Before Mom. https://bertmanderson.com/100-positive-affirmations-mom/

Dior, C. (2020, November 14). *37 Affirmations for Black Moms* «. Personal Growth Blog and Coaching for Black Women. http://fromcaterpillarstobutterflies.com/lifestyle/37-affirmations-for-black-moms/

Horton, S. (2020, October 28). *73 Positive Affirmations to Liberate Moms Who Feel Overwhelmed*. Motherhood Sprouting. https://motherhoodsprouting.com/73-positive-affirmations-to-liberate-moms-who-feel-overwhelmed/

M. (2021, February 9). *42 Positive Affirmations for Moms to Help Reduce Anxiety, Increase Positivity & Energy.* Momalot. https://momalot.com/42-positive-affirmations-for-moms/

Perez, D. (2021, June 23). *50 Motivating and Powerful Affirmations for Moms –.* Wild Simple Joy. https://wildsimplejoy.com/affirmations-mama-life/

Tamm, L. (2021, January 13). *How Positive Affirmations Change My Mindset on the Really Hard Mom Days.* The Military Wife and Mom. https://themilitarywifeandmom.com/brilliant-positive-affirmations-for-moms/

Tuttle, C. (2021, August 13). *68 affirmations that'll empower you to be the parent you want to be.* Motherly. https://www.mother.ly/life/youve-got-this-68-affirmations-to-use-to-become-the-parent-you-want-to-be